T0008812

p

Checks and Balances

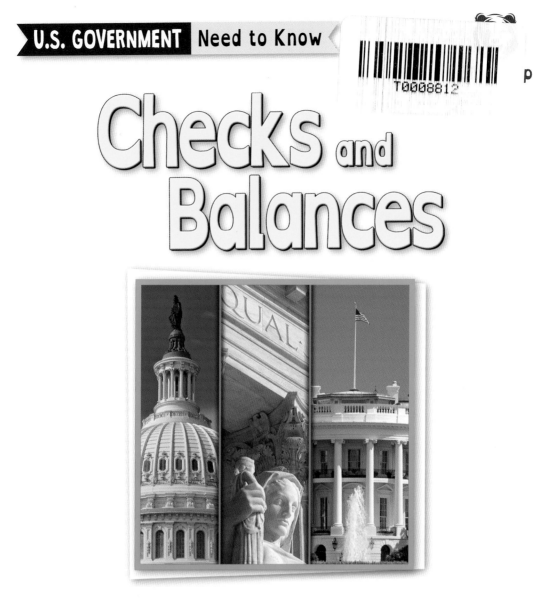

by Karen Latchana Kenney

Consultant: John Coleman
Professor of Political Science, University of Minnesota
Minneapolis, Minnesota

BEARPORT
PUBLISHING

Minneapolis, Minnesota

Credits

Cover and Title Page, © Bob Korn/Shutterstock, © Vacclav/iStock, and © Orhan Cam/Shutterstock; 3, © Dan Thornberg/Shutterstock; 5T, © Andru Goldman/Shutterstock; 5M, © David Evison/ Shutterstock; 5B, © Brandon Bourdages/Shutterstock; 6–7, © Orhan Cam/Shutterstock; 9, © javarman/ Shutterstock; 11, © The White House/Getty; 13, © Wojciech Stróżyk/Alamy; 15, © Pool/Getty; 17, © Chip Somodevilla /Getty; 19, © Mark Wilson/Getty; 21, © Joshua Roberts/Getty; 23, © Robert Alexander / Getty; 25, © Bettmann /Getty; 27, © fstop123/iStock; 28, © Gennady_Sokolov/Shutterstock, © kmsdesen/ Shutterstock, and © stas11/Shutterstock.

President: Jen Jenson
Director of Product Development: Spencer Brinker
Senior Editor: Allison Juda
Associate Editor: Charly Haley
Senior Designer: Colin O'Dea

Library of Congress Cataloging-in-Publication Data

Names: Kenney, Karen Latchana, author.
Title: Checks and balances / by Karen Latchana Kenney.
Description: Silvertip Books. | Minneapolis, Minnesota : Bearport
    Publishing Company, [2022] | Series: U.S. Government: Need to Know | Includes
    bibliographical references and index.
Identifiers: LCCN 2021034168 (print) | LCCN 2021034169 (ebook) | ISBN
    9781636915975 (Library Binding) | ISBN 9781636916040 (Paperback) | ISBN
    9781636916118 (eBook)
Subjects: LCSH: Separation of powers—United States. | United
    States—Politics and government.
Classification: LCC JK305 .K4 2022 (print) | LCC JK305 (ebook) | DDC
    320.473—dc23
LC record available at https://lccn.loc.gov/2021034168
LC ebook record available at https://lccn.loc.gov/2021034169

Copyright © 2022 Bearport Publishing Company. All rights reserved. No part of this publication may be reproduced in whole or in part, stored in any retrieval system, or transmitted in any form or by any means, electronic, mechanical, photocopying, recording, or otherwise, without written permission from the publisher.

For more information, write to Bearport Publishing, 5357 Penn Avenue South, Minneapolis, MN 55419. Printed in the United States of America.

Contents

A Smart System

In the United States, lawmakers can't pass laws alone. Many people decide who will be a judge. And the head of the country doesn't just do whatever they want. Our government was set up this way for a reason. It keeps powers divided. It's the system of checks and balances.

America's founders were careful not to give any one person too much power. They didn't want a government like the one they had just left. There, kings and queens had the power.

EQUAL·JUSTICE·UNDER·LAW

Parts and Powers

Government powers are divided between three branches, or parts. The **legislative** branch makes laws. It says what people can and cannot do. The **executive** branch makes sure laws are carried out. And the **judicial** branch decides the meaning of laws.

All three branches of the **federal government** meet in Washington, D.C.

The president leads the executive branch. The legislative branch is made of the House of Representatives and the Senate. Together, they are called Congress. And the Supreme Court is at the top of the judicial branch.

The system of checks and balances is key to our government. It keeps any one branch from having too much control. Many people across branches have to agree. The branches balance, or share, power. And they check by setting limits on one another.

The idea of checks and balances wasn't new in the United States. In ancient Rome, the government had three main parts. Ancient Greek historian Polybius also impacted how we think about dividing up a government.

Parts of ancient Rome still stand today. So do some of their thoughts about government!

Making Laws

So, how does the system work? You can see it in action with federal laws. Different branches have a say over laws.

Laws start as bills in the legislative branch. Both parts of Congress need to agree on a bill. They check one another.

The House has 435 voting members. The Senate has 100. A **majority** in each part of Congress needs to agree for a bill to pass.

Sometimes, members of the House and the Senate meet to make laws.

After Congress passes a bill, it goes to the executive branch. The president can sign the bill to make it a law. Or they can **veto** the bill to stop it.

Laws that have passed can also be stopped by the judicial branch. Courts can decide a law is not allowed.

Even if the president vetoes a bill, it doesn't stop there. The bill goes back to the legislative branch. If two-thirds of Congress vote to approve it, the bill becomes a law.

Orders from the President

What if a president wants to get things done without Congress? They can make **executive orders**. These orders have a lot of the same powers as laws. But they come from the president.

Even executive orders can be stopped, though. The court can say they are not allowed, just like laws.

President Franklin D. Roosevelt made 3,721 executive orders. That is the most of any president. William Henry Harrison was the only president not to make any orders. He died after one month in office.

Joe Biden made more than 60 orders in his first 100 days as president.

The Power to Choose

The courts have a lot of power to stop laws and executive orders. But they do not stand alone. In fact, the executive branch has powers over the judicial branch. The president is in charge of picking federal judges. In this way, a president may impact the courts by picking certain judges.

There are many courts in the judicial branch. And there are a lot of judges. Many presidents pick more than 100 judges during their time in office.

Presidents get to pick judges as high up as those on the Supreme Court.

The legislative branch can also affect the courts. After a president picks the judges they want, the Senate has the final say. So, senators can say no to a president's choice. In this way, all branches are balancing power.

Senators study if a judge will be a good fit for the Supreme Court. They look at the judge's history. They ask the judge questions. Then, they vote on the judge.

A Supreme Court judge needs to answer questions before Congress in order to be approved.

The President's People

When they come into power, the president also picks people to help them run the government. They are members of the president's **cabinet**. These people lead different parts of the government.

But the Senate has final say over cabinet choices, too. Sometimes, they say no to the president's picks, just like with judges.

In U.S. history, the Senate has said no to nine people chosen for the cabinet. President John Tyler had the most people turned down. The Senate did not accept four of his choices.

Michael Regan is part of
President Joe Biden's cabinet.

You're Out!

What if someone already in office does something wrong? Congress can **impeach** some other members of the government.

The **House** charges the person. Then, the **Senate** holds a trial. With enough votes in the Senate, a judge or even the president may lose their job.

In 1868, Andrew Johnson was the first president to be impeached. Many people did not like what he did after the Civil War (1861–1865).

Donald Trump was the most recent president to be impeached.

Going to War

This system even works to impact how the United States behaves with other countries. There are checks and balances for times of war. The president is in charge of the U.S. military. But the president cannot start a war. The legislative branch holds that responsibility.

The last time Congress declared war was in 1942. President Franklin D. Roosevelt asked them to do so. It sent the United States into World War II (1939–1945).

President Roosevelt's speech moved Congress to enter the United States into World War II.

Spreading the Power

Many other checks and balances were put into our government from the very start. America's founders always wanted to spread government power between many people. This means more people can help make our country fair for all. That's the power of checks and balances.

There are even checks for the federal government as a whole. It only has some of the power. Other powers belong to states and the people.

Checks and Balances

The three branches of the federal government share powers.

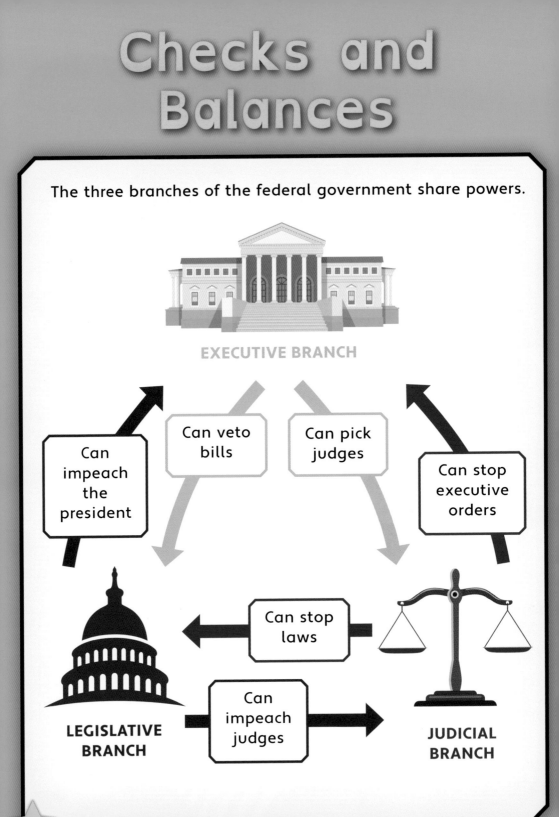

EXECUTIVE BRANCH

Can impeach the president

Can veto bills

Can pick judges

Can stop executive orders

Can stop laws

Can impeach judges

LEGISLATIVE BRANCH

JUDICIAL BRANCH

★ SilverTips for REVIEW

Review what you've learned. Use the text to help you.

Define key terms

bill

judges

executive order

veto

impeach

Check for understanding

What are the three branches of government?

Describe one power for each branch of government and one way each branch has their power checked.

What was the reason for setting up a system of checks and balances in the United States government?

Think deeper

How do checks and balances impact the people of the United States? Name at least one example.

★ SilverTips on TEST-TAKING

★ **Make a study plan.** Ask your teacher what the test is going to cover. Then, set aside time to study a little bit every day.

★ **Read all the questions carefully.** Be sure you know what is being asked.

★ **Skip any questions** you don't know how to answer right away. Mark them and come back later if you have time.

Glossary

cabinet a group of people who give advice to the leader of a government

executive related to the branch of government that includes the president and vice president

executive orders rules made by the president that have similar power as laws

federal having to do with the government of a nation

impeach to charge someone who holds public office with a crime

judicial related to the branch of government that includes courts and judges

legislative related to the branch of government with people who make laws

majority a number that is more than half of the total group

veto the power of a person to decide that something will not be approved

Read More

Faust, Daniel R. *Separation of Powers (Rosen Verified: U.S. Government)*. New York: Rosen Publishing, 2021.

Krasner, Barbara. *Exploring Checks and Balances (Searchlight Books: Getting into Government)*. Minneapolis: Lerner Publications, 2020.

Lawton, Cassie. *Checks and Balances (The Inside Guide: Civics)*. New York: Cavendish Square Publishing, 2021.

Learn More Online

1. Go to **www.factsurfer.com** or scan the QR code below.

2. Enter "**Checks and Balances**" into the search box.

3. Click on the cover of this book to see a list of websites.

Index

About the Author

Karen Latchana Kenney is an author and editor. She lives in Minnetonka, MN.